The Model's Bible

The Model's Bible

By RC Lane

The Model's Bible

To the Professional Model Within You . . .

The Model's Bible

Contents

Introduction

Modeling is an occupation many dream of and few ever realize at a successful level. Bringing this reality about requires heart and perseverance through a lot of trying times. Times that can also take you to places in the world you would have never imagined being, bring you large sums of cash for a relatively easy day's worth of work, and allow you to make lifelong friends all over the world. Modeling is more than a job, it is an adventure and can help to facilitate growth from places within yourself you thought unreachable. All the traveling and meeting new people really helps to expand your perspective of the world we live in. Persevere, never accept someone saying that you cannot achieve something and one day you may find yourself in front of the camera, living your dreams.

The best way to succeed is to know what kind of potential you really have and what markets you would have the likeliest chance of working in, even if you don't consider yourself high fashion model material. Depending on the trends of the industry, your look just might be the next big thing.

Upon starting out in this industry, you will quickly learn firsthand what to avoid and what to familiarize yourself with. Learning how to adapt to a changing environment is a very important skill as a model. Every job is going to be much different from the last, which helps to keep things from feeling stagnant but, also requires that you are working with an entirely different crew every time you are on set. It is possible that, on occasion, you may run in to people you know on set but, for the most part, you are always either working with different people, casting with different people, or on a different location. How well you learn to adapt to changing environments can be the deciding factor in the level of success you experience within the industry.

Modeling is not your typical 9 to 5 job. Often times the so called glamour is very demanding and sacrifices must be made. Look forward to rising with the sun or watching it rise depending on the shoot. Eighteen hour days are very common as well. Along with the fabulousness of the job also comes responsibility and commitment. Airports, hotels, and jetlag will become your best friends as you develop your career and start to work consistently, not to say that these things are not all equally loveable in their own ways. Most of the traveling is typically done alone, excluding fashion week. Don't worry; sometimes this can be a good thing.

Traveling alone develops a sense of independence and worldliness that cannot be created otherwise. Crossing oceans and mountains, coming back, hopefully unscathed from your adventures, allows you to see that you are capable of anything and gives you the confidence to try new things.

Belief in yourself is the most important ingredient in accomplishing anything worthwhile; becoming a successful model is no different. You will face rejection every day, even once you become established in the industry. Being able to deal with these supposed setbacks in a healthy way is a very important quality in a professional model. Developing faith in yourself and a bit of thick skin are the most important aspects of becoming successful in any facet of the entertainment industry. Just remember, every "no" that you hear gets you closer to a "yes". Sometimes careers happen overnight and sometimes they take a little while to materialize, but you have to be in it to win it so, one foot after the other.

The experience I draw on comes from working in the capitals of fashion since my career began over a decade ago. It has been my good fortune to have worked with some of the world's best photographers for some of the most prestigious fashion houses and magazine clients including Calvin Klein, Dolce & Gabbana, Lancôme, Maybelline, Vogue, Harper's Bazaar, and many others. I have spent six seasons on the high fashion runways of Milan, Paris, and New York for some of the biggest designers in the industry including John Varvatos, Calvin Klein, Exte, Dolce & Gabbana, D'Squared, and Valentino.

This book was written in an effort to help people accomplish their dreams in the most efficient way possible by passing on the knowledge I have gained through personal experience. The collection of experiences found in the pages ahead of you can help you to take the steps in the right direction toward a rewarding career as a model. Believe me when I say, I have been right where you are now. Trying to discover an angle on how to break in to the business and make it to the top in the smallest amount of time possible. It is my hope for you that this information will somehow give you a better perspective of where you might best fit in to this world and how to succeed once there.

Modeling has been a blessing that has changed my life in more ways than, I am sure, I am presently aware. A wise man once said, "It's great work if you can get it," and I am here to help you gain as much knowledge as possible in order to get it. If you follow the advice found in the chapters ahead, you will be able to step on set with the knowledge necessary to be the best model you can possibly be. Learn the basics, work hard, and reap the rewards.

Chapter 1: Evaluate Your Product

Upon entering into a market it is extremely important to define what category of model you represent and be well aware of what you have to offer the agencies that cater to your specific look. Let's step outside ourselves here and really think about this objectively for a moment. This is a business and you are, however you want to look at it, a marketable product. What category of the market do you see yourself being cast in? There are six categories to choose from which I will cover in detail below: editorial/high fashion, commercial modeling, runway modeling, child modeling, plus size modeling, and fit modeling.

Do you have a very distinct face? High fashion and editorial clients love unique faces with highly defined bone structure, something that stands out from the crowd. Classically beautiful faces are also beginning to work well within these markets. Could be your eyes, cheek bones, whatever defines you. In the industry we call these people editorial models, or high fashion models. These are the people that you see in the high profile campaigns and commercials for Calvin Klein, Gucci, and Gap such as Kate Moss, Naomi Campbell, Jessica Stam, Tyson Ballou, Noah Mills, and David Gandy.

This market definitely has the most monetary potential for a model. However, don't expect to make a lot of money only doing editorial work. Most models you see in magazines were paid very little to be in the magazine itself. The real benefit of editorial work comes from working with great photographers who will eventually do money jobs and hopefully remember you when they do. Editorial work also offers a good deal of exposure and helps you to build your portfolio in order to book more work. When doing editorial work, you should expect to be paid no more than $200 with the possible benefit of travel to a cool location with your hotel and food paid for. Not too shabby.

The real money in high fashion modeling is found in fragrance and beauty contracts with some of the larger designers. With these jobs you can expect to make anywhere from $30K up into the seven figure range. Of course this is all contingent on the designer and the terms of the contract.

Catalog work is where you can expect to make the day to day money as a model. Some top models command day rates of up to $50K. Of course these are the supermodels like

Kate Moss and other women bordering on household names. Men can always expect to make a little less. A top male model can get up to $20K a day with certain clients. The average is around $5K. Hopefully you can find yourself doing all of these jobs which is how to really stack the dough as a model.

If you have the suitable body dimensions designers will employ you in order to fit their sample clothing to your body. This is a very quiet niche within the industry and most of the working fit models will never be seen in a magazine or campaign. However it is not uncommon for fit models to make upward of $250K/ year. In a perfect world, you can hop back and forth between this type of work and high fashion. This area of the modeling industry is called Fit Modeling. The required measurements are very specific, usually 5'6" - 5'8" for women and 6' - 6'3" for men. The specific dimensions required usually vary depending on the client/designer you will be working for. Patience is a virtue when it comes to this type of modeling as you will be required to stand for hours on end without doing or saying much at all.

Commercial modeling requires a more everyday kind of look from models and the clients employing you will be less high fashion based or not fashion based at all. Most big agencies have a division of the company dedicated to representing commercial models. This board is often referred to as the lifestyle board. This sort of modeling often pays a little less than more high profile fashion jobs but, there tends to be more work available and therefore can be more consistently booked. Consistent earnings in the modeling world are a god send and more and more of a rarity in the post-recession industry. Some models can jump back and forth between the commercial and high fashion clients. Remember, the name of the game is versatility when it comes to having a long term career.

Plus size modeling is also a very lucrative part of the industry for men and women, mostly women, who have a larger body dimensions. Fashion designers are starting to look more closely at the earning potential from plus-size clothing, and have used plus-size models for their advertising campaigns and catwalks. Jean-Paul Gaultier and John Galliano both used plus-size models in their Spring 2006 showings in Paris. Gaultier also used plus- size models Marquita Pring and Crystal Renn in his Spring 2011 Ready to Wear show. Italian plus-size fashion house Elena Mirò now regularly stages biannual prêt-à-porter shows during Fashion Week in Milan. Mark Fast and William Tempest each used plus-size models during their own London Fashion Week showings for Spring 2009, and again as part of All Walks Beyond the Catwalk event held on 19 September 2009 in association with the British Fashion Council. Mark Fast also used plus-size models in Fall 2010, Fall 2011, and Spring 2012.

Most of the larger modeling agencies have a division

dedicated to the representation of plus size models and there are specialty agencies that only represent plus size models and work exclusively with plus size clients.

Runway modeling is also a facet of the industry for models to consider. Ideally, runway modeling will be just a part of your career as a model. Most high fashion models, both men and women, are also runway models and dedicate themselves twice a year to appearing in fashion shows in Milan, Paris, and New York City. Like editorial work, most runway shows do not pay a great deal of money unless you are a top model or you are booked exclusively to walk for a single designer.

Runway shows and fashion week in general should be viewed as a way to gain exposure in the industry as most of the magazine editors, photographers, agents and designers will be in attendance. Walking in the shows is a great way to get your face out there. Women, as usual, can expect to make a lot more money during fashion week. Most of getting booked for runway shows has to do with having the proper measurements for the designers clothing. Obviously possessing a unique look and an established position within the industry doesn't hurt either. If you are planning on only working as runway model, I would not count on making a lot of money as this work is seasonal and can tend to vary on the rates paid.

If you are the parent of an adorable youngster, there are a lot of opportunities to get them working at a young age. Most agencies, even smaller regional agencies will have a children's board representing a number of youngsters. However, as a parent be prepared to go through all the motions of a working model with your child. You will be required to drive them to their castings and photo shoots and will be there with them for the duration. The hours on set are usually kept to a minimum for children to accommodate their attention span. After a few jobs as child model, you could be well on your way to having college or a sweet sixteen car paid for. Some child models even become fixtures themselves within the industry and can earn a good living at a young age. However, this is the exception, not the rule.

It is very important you establish what market best suits you early on and discuss your perception with any potential agency you might be considering signing with. Otherwise you end up spinning your wheels and becoming very frustrated with the matter. To make the most of your career you should try to focus on whatever markets will best utilize your look. Keep in mind, the more diversified you can market yourself as, the more chances you have of being successful in multiple markets.

Chapter 2: Getting an Agency

So, by now you have successfully established what you have to offer and where you best fit in this whacky world. What's next you ask? Time to get the ball rolling by evaluating agencies and deciding which one best suits your current needs as a model.

We are going to start at the top; New York City, where the cream of the modeling crop resides. The idea is, if you get with a reputable New York City based agency, all the agencies in other markets will perceive you as being a higher caliber model and be more willing to work with you as you expand your agency range into other markets. All the major campaigns and advertising projects are cast from the advertising agencies and photo representatives located within the city. Therefore it is very beneficial to live in a city with a major market early on in your career, if possible. I know this won't be possible for a lot of people, just a suggestion. Don't worry it's not a deal breaker. Check out the top five New York agencies. If you are fortunate enough to live in the city, call them up and ask what day and time they have open calls. Agencies are always recruiting new faces and this is the time they have reserved to meet prospective models.

Say that you are geographically isolated and don't have the ability to travel to an agency's open call casting. Don't sweat it; all you need to do is get a friend to take a few digital shots of you. Sometimes these shots are referred to as Polaroid's in the industry. However, with the advent of digital, no one really uses them anymore. One being a full length shot to get the idea of your body type and three headshots that features your sexy mug from a full frontal perspective and two from three quarters profile. Keep the clothing and background simple. If you are submitting to be a high fashion model you should include a shot of yourself in a two piece bathing suit as a woman and a pair of simple briefs if you are a man. More and more clients are beginning to book classically fit men and women. Stand against a simple white wall with the lighting in front of you. Natural lighting best highlights your features and makes it a lot easier for the prospective agent to get an idea of what you really look like as a person. The bells and whistles of professional photography will come later. Makeup should be kept to a minimal as agents want to get an idea of how you naturally look.

Next get the email address of your chosen agencies, preferably the agent's direct email, and send the digital photographs in along with all your measurements and contact information. Most agencies will display an email address to contact the specific division of the agency on their website. Keep it short and sweet. No life stories here. If you're signed, you will have plenty of time to cover all of that later. Contact information should include full name, address, both home and cell phone number, and email address. Measurements should include height, suit, shirt, waist, inseam, shoe, hair color and eye color. Women should also include bust and dress size, respectively. This process is relatively painless compared to spending loads of cash on a test photographer before you even have representation.

Remember the work I was talking about earlier, this is where it comes in to play. In the beginning it is good policy to compile a list of the top five agencies in New York City and send all of them your digital shots. Allow approximately one week for the shots to arrive and be reviewed by the agents. Most likely the agency will contact you if they are interested. However, this is not always the case, agencies are busy places and yes, they are human and sometimes things fall through the cracks. Give them a call as a friendly reminder just to make sure that everyone is on the same page and to confirm they received the images. No need for discouragement if you do not sign with the first agency you contact. New York City is full of excellent agencies all having different requirements for the models they represent. You are marketing yourself in this industry; you must push until you can push no more. Sooner or later someone will want to take a chance on you and things will come together.

Upon meeting your prospective agents always remember, having confidence, not to be mistaken with arrogance, is key. Nothing is sexier than a person who has confidence and is comfortable with themselves. This is your chance to talk with the agents face to face and get an idea of what a business relationship would be like. Find out what clients the agency works with, how many models they represent, what percentages of money are taken from what you earn, and how their system of payment works. Ask to speak with models that are currently signed to the agency about their experiences working with the agency. Use this time you have with the agent to just have a normal conversation and feel their energy as humans. You will be working very closely together for some time to come. Remember, sign with someone you like as a person. Just because someone is working at a huge agency does not necessarily mean you should sign with them. Sign with the person you get along with. It will make life as a model much easier.

Depending on your look and how developed your portfolio is, early on it could be detrimental to your career to sign with a huge agency. Not always but, this is something to keep in mind in the beginning. Sometimes young models just get swallowed up on a large board with tons of established faces due to the lack of work in their books. Again, this is not the norm but, just a thought to keep in mind.

There are two things to consider when making the decision to go with an agency, what a good agent can bring to the table and what a bad agent can take away. Be objective in your decision making and manage this situation like you would any other business decision. Do not go with someone that you feel only wants to subject you to their inferiority complex. Ideally you want someone representing you who has a personal interest in seeing you develop and progress in your career as a model. It is very important that you interview with a number of agencies before selecting the one that will be representing you. Remember, you need an agent that is going to pay close attention to managing your career. Not someone who is going to sell you short of your potential.

If for some reason you find yourself well into your lists of prospective agencies and without a contract offer, don't panic. This is how it goes. Agencies differ in the look they are representing as the trends in the industry begin to shift and sometimes it really is a matter of timing. Persevere in your search until something positive happens. There are a lot of really successful models that did not get signed immediately upon arriving in New York City. Also, it is not imperative that you find representation in New York City immediately. If an agency does not offer a contract, you can always look in other markets such as Los Angeles, Miami, and Chicago.

Older men and women, along with parents that have children, should look to the nearest major market and start meeting with agencies that represent child models and senior models. If you cannot travel to make the open call dates, you should follow the same digital photo procedure listed above. Do your research and start with the most reputable agency that you are able to find and work your way down the chain until you find an agency you feel comfortable working with.

Agents, not all agents, will sometimes give constructive criticism upon your meeting them, whether you ask for it or not. Use your best judgment when adhering to this advice. Take the bulk with a grain of salt and do what you can. Never put your health in harms way for modeling, it's just not worth it in the end. They may ask you to lose weight, gain weight, cut your hair, grow your hair, get a tan, stay out of the sun, etc… and most of the time it will be a different critique from agent to agent. Again, grain of salt. If it sounds sensible and reasonable, go with it. If not, forget it and move on.

When an agency offers you a contract there are a few standard and appropriate points to clarify. The first is always commission. It is vital to understand the commission the agency will be taking from the jobs they will be booking you on. Twenty percent (20%) is the standard agency commission rate. Some models reach a level of stardom that creates leveraging power for them and can consequently negotiate a lower commission rate. Twenty percent (20%) is generally the standard though. Secondly, you should never sign with an agency for more than a year at a time. Some contracts lock models in for three years or more. This is a bad idea, especially in the beginning, because you will be stuck no matter what. Even if the agency turns out to be not such a great fit for you as a model, you will be forced to wait it out and waste valuable time. Most agencies should be fine with an annual contract. If things are rocking along and you are working consistently in your chosen niche of the industry, then by all means, when the time comes, sign on for another year.

There is a common misconception about all modeling start up costs encountered early on in a career being paid for by the agency. This is not quite the case. If an agency thinks that they can make money with you, they will front you all the cash needed to start your career, everything ranging from, plane tickets to New York City to meet clients, to a place to stay in the city while you are casting for jobs, building a portfolio, to printing composite cards. However, all these expenses will go on record with the agency and you will be responsible for paying them back at a later time when you begin to work. Being in debt to an agency is often referred to as being in the black. The lighter side of this is that you are using other people's money to fund the start up costs of your career. Don't worry about this though.

Agencies are in business for a reason and they would not be spending the money if they were not confident that a nice return was in hot pursuit. Plus, if you are in debt to them they tend to work a little harder so you can pay it off quickly.

Most agencies also hold what is often referred to as a "model's apartment". This is an apartment owned or leased by an agency and then subleased out to models for a short time while they are in town on a shoot or seeing clients. Model's apartments are a good way to expand your client range without breaking the bank early on.

Chapter 3: Building a Portfolio

Let me start by saying, you do not need to build a portfolio in order to get signed with an agency. I have seen a lot of people spend thousands of dollars having professional photos taken only to see them get tossed in the garbage upon signing with an agency. Let the agency refer you to a photographer if you are going to pay for a test shoot. Just to be certain you know what we are talking about when we say portfolio, a portfolio is a book consisting of your most appealing pictures you carry with you to all your castings. At the casting, you will present your portfolio to the clients and leave a composite card with them as well, often referred to as just a "card".

Upon signing with an agency it is important to seek out budding photographers in order to "test" and build a solid foundation of pictures in your portfolio. The fact is, in the beginning you don't know which agency you will end up with and what markets you will primarily be working within. You may end up wasting money if you test with a photographer before you have an agency. This will not always be the case but agencies will have a list of budding photographers who are trying to build their books as well. If you wait until after you get an agency you will hopefully end up testing for free. The photographer your agency sets you up with should best represent your unique look with his style of photography. Your agent should be able to point you to some of these people pretty easily using their connections. If this does not turn out to be the case, the Internet is an excellent way to connect with other artists. Look for photographers willing to work for a trade agreement. However, it is a good idea to meet with the photographer before the shoot in order to create a vision of the final outcome of the shoot. It's okay to bring someone along for safety. Planning the shoot is very critical. Skip it and you might spend a lot of time taking pictures you will never use.

Another great thing about shooting with young up and coming photographers is that some day they will be the old photographers who are shooting all the big campaigns. Most of my career has been built from working with up and coming photographers in the beginning and then re-uniting for a major label or fragrance gig later on. It is from these test shoots that you can take your book to prospective clients and say, "I am the model for this job." Remember that every top model has taken a thousand bad pictures but, clients never see those in the book. You need only have the shots in your book that you truly believe in and have a real connection to. Otherwise, you will dread showing them to clients and you need all the confidence and charisma you can gather walking into those rooms. Good portfolios are very diverse in the emotion displayed throughout the photos. Being sexy and seductive is definitely a good thing but, remember that you should be diverse as possible in your test. This will enable you to put together a more complete representation of yourself. Place the strongest picture first and the second strongest being the last shot of the book. A lot of times castings are hectic and clients are in a hurry to get through each interview. In this arrangement you optimize your time with them and leave on a positive note.

A composite card generally consists of four to five of your best shots; it is essentially a smaller representation of your portfolio and will act as a sort of business card. Basically, something that enables the clients to get a feel for your look at a glance. There will be a pocket at the back of your portfolio holding these cards so that clients can easily access them after looking over your book. One large photo should be on the front along with your name and agency logo in a position not distracting from your face. Then two or three photos on the back side along with all your measurements and agency contact information usually located somewhere near the bottom.

Larger agencies have in house printers able to print, not only composite cards but, pictures for your book as well. You will generally get a good deal if this is the case. Smaller agencies will most often send you to an independent print shop to have the composites and prints made. The standard measurements for portfolio quality prints are 9.5" x 12"; this size best fits the laminated sleeves of the standard portfolio.

Always carry your book with you when you leave the house and make certain there is an ample supply of comp cards in the back pocket. Models are literally on call most of the time. Things happen very fast in major markets at the larger agencies. Clients are calling from all over the world at all hours of the night. You never know when an opportunity is going to arise so be prepared.

Chapter 4: What to Expect at a Casting

As a working model you will be required to pound the
pavement day in and day out meeting prospective clients,
casting for your next job. How this is done is relatively
simple. You will be sent on castings, quick job interviews,
which allow the client to get a feel for who you are. Most of
the time an advertising agency or casting director will phone
a modeling agency on behalf of a client and request a certain
type of look for a casting, be it, dark, light, quirky, classic,
muscular, androgynous, older, younger, whatever. Every
client is different in the look they are seeking for their
campaign.

The agent then puts together a package of all the composite
cards of the models they think might fit the look for that
particular job. The client then receives the package, sifts
through the composite cards, and requests to meet the
models that most suit the look they are going for. The agent

then adds the casting to what is called your "chart", or schedule, for the week. At the end of the day you should always "check in" with the agency to make sure that you have all the information for the castings that are being held the next day.

If you don't have an email account it would be a good idea to get one. This is how much of the casting information will be transferred. Castings are often done face to face and are a great chance for you to show the client a little of what you have to offer. Upon arriving always check to see if there is a sign in sheet, the list of people in the order they arrived, sign it as soon as you get there in order to save yourself some time and confusion. Often times you will find these at open castings, better known as cattle calls. If you fail to sign in, you won't have any idea of when your turn is and could end up wasting a lot of time. Wait your turn and when the time comes, just breathe and be yourself, not the ideal you think the client is expecting. I see a lot of people go in to the meetings trying to be super macho or too sexy and hard to get. It doesn't work. Most of the time it will only come off as obnoxious or insecure. The important thing to remember is that these people are humans too, so be yourself.

Clients respond to sincerity and humor just as anyone would. They are looking for someone with charisma and personality who they wouldn't mind hanging out with for a couple of days on set. Obviously, don't go in and throw your feet on the desk or anything like that, but going in completely nervous or over-zealous will get you nowhere fast.

Depending on the nature of the casting, you will be asked to try on some of the products, the client will look through your book, take a card, and a series of digital photos and possibly a few minutes of video will be taken. Digital photos allow the client to see what you look like without Photoshop. Also, don't feel disappointed if the casting agent does not burst with joy upon seeing your book or keep you for hours chatting about whatever. These people are hired for their ability to be objective and keep the client, and their product, in mind when choosing the talent, so just do the best you can and then put it in the back of your mind. Way back in the back. After you walk away from the casting put it in the back of your mind, sit tight and see. That's all you can do. Ask my agent, I have driven myself, and him, to the brink of insanity thinking about that job just hanging on the board, calling him up every five minutes to check on the option.

Throughout your career big options will come and they will go. Hopefully some of them will materialize and naturally, some of them will die as options. That's the name of the game. Ninety percent of modeling is rejection, you will hear "no" many more times than you will hear "yes". However, one "yes" is worth a thousand "no's" and can make all the difference in your career.

One thing to keep in mind upon entering this world, there is really no such thing as competition in modeling. Yes, people will seem competitive and sometimes downright bitchy but, in the end, you can only present what you have to offer and allow the clients to decide. Your face and body will always be your face and body. There is no rhyme or reason to what type of look will be successful in modeling. It is literally an industry based on the taste and whims of a small number of people. That is not to say that the hard work as a model does not get you further than someone who does not work hard. The models who are always traveling to different markets and stay in contact with their agencies and dedicate themselves to attending fashion week every season are definitely in a much better position to succeed long term.

Lastly, if the client sees you as a valid candidate for the job you will be placed on hold, meaning you are, at the moment, being highly considered for the job, along with any number of other models. Options are a nice step in the right direction but, take them for what they are, options. When and if the client decides you have the image they are looking to associate with their product you will be confirmed for the booking. After the confirmation, follows the negotiation of the rate, details of the shoot, usage, location, and flight information. All of this will be handled by your agent and relayed to you as soon as possible. A good agent is going for, either the most exposure, or the most money they can possibly get for you on any job you are hired for.

Chapter 5: Your Role as a Model and the Anatomy of a Photo Shoot

Now comes the fun part, working on a professional photo set. This is the moment you have been working so hard for. So, let's familiarize ourselves with the different job titles involved in a photo shoot and where you fit in as a model. Before we get in to that, let's talk about the right attitude going into a job. The right attitude is absolutely key to getting rebooked and enjoying a long term career. A lot of people step on set thinking the shoot revolves around them. Not the case, although a big part of the production, a model is not the sun around which the shoot revolves. It is always best to go into a photo shoot having realized you are part of a larger equation and the more you cooperate and strive to be a true professional, the more likely you are to become a success. Remember, it's not about working with a client once then moving on. The word of the day is, "rebook". It is vitally important to develop friendships and work well with people in order to not be a flash in the pan. Hard work and sincerity will never go unnoticed in anything you do, modeling is no exception.

Now for the breakdown of the aforementioned equation comprising the set, by better understanding the roles of others you can become a more productive model and, as a result, make more money. Let's go ahead and discuss the set of an advertising campaign.

These are most likely the most complex sets you will encounter and that utilize every component a professional shoot has to offer. I was shocked when I showed up in Mexico on the set of Calvin Klein and saw the small army they had flown in. Remember, everyone on set plays an equal and vital role in this process.

Starting with the producer, this person is the maestro of the shoot. The producer is the person who gathers all the components of the shoot into one happy family for the day to get the job done. Usually employed by the ad agency to make sure the shoot happens on time, according to preset guidelines. Producers are vital to a production running smoothly, as they are the ones that solve unplanned problems on set, help to find locations and generally make certain everyone is doing the best job they can at all times. The producer is the person that will be signing your voucher at the end of the day. The voucher system allows the billing process to be much more efficient. Vouchers must be signed at the end of every shoot; this allows the agency to verify that the job was, in fact, finished and provides the information needed to bill the client.

Moving on to the artistic director, this person is usually brought in by the clients to keep the shoot following one artistic vision. Artistic directors are employed to work very closely with the photographer, stylist, make up, and hair to ensure the shoot has a theme and is moving in the right direction according the needs of the brand. The theme and direction of the shoot is always a collaboration but, the artistic director is the only person specifically hired to oversee it.

The composer of the set is the photographer. The set and job will really dictate how much creative control a photographer has. Editorial shoots for magazine spreads will almost always be led by a photographer. The stature of a photographer will also dictate how much creative control they have outside of an editorial job. Bigger photographers have long relationships with certain fashion houses and are given relative freedom to construct a campaign the way they see fit. Younger photographers and photographers who shoot exclusively for catalog clients tend to be given less reign creatively on set.

As a model you must develop the sensitivity of an artist to be able to create more in tune with the vision of the photographer you are working with. Trust their vision but don't be afraid to speak up about your own ideas or ask questions so as to better understand the image they are trying to capture. It's always a good idea to ask the photographer what sort of feeling they are envisioning for the shot. This allows you to create more in tune with the overall goal of the shoot. Bottom line, if you can consistently deliver images they can use, you will begin to be regarded as a commodity within the industry. This is the only way to develop your career to the level at which you are trusted with larger budget jobs and rewarded appropriately.

A high level photographer usually has two to three assistants at work alongside them on set. These are men and women who help to load film, test lighting, and make certain that a high level of productivity is maintained throughout the day. Often times these individuals are talented up and comers honing their craft and gaining hands on experience working with the masters.

Depending on the vision of the shoot and complexity of the set a set designer may be employed. In which case, they will bring with them anything necessary to facilitate the photographer and his goal for the day. I remember laughing hysterically when I looked inside the back of David LaChapelle's prop truck and saw ceremonial Indian head dresses, life sized plastic horses and some shiny purple cowboy chaps. I thought to myself, "This should make for an interesting afternoon, wonder if there are any leprechauns, in there? What if I find a leprechaun in there? Would I tell anybody or just quietly beat the location of the gold out him?" We ended up in the middle of the Bellagio in Las Vegas with a baffled crowd watching us surrounding the set.

Stylists are the people that show up on set carrying the real star of the show, the clothes. Clothes are to a stylist as what paint is to a painter. Their job is making sure that the clothes fit the mood of the shoot depending on what the photographer and client are going for. The client basically comes to the stylist with a vague idea or reference to a look and feel and it is the stylist's job to interpret that request and bring it to life. Throughout the day they will be pinning, stretching, and changing your clothing. Believe me, after 15 hours on set it can start to wear thin. Hang in there and be cool, this is their job, allow them to experiment with the clothes and maintain a professional attitude. Once you are wearing the clothes that will be photographed, do yourself a favor and don't sit down. Sitting wrinkles everything and the stylist might stab you. As well, it is not a good idea to eat, drink, or smoke anything while you are in their clothes.

Makeup artist are hired to make sure that the model looks absolutely flawless throughout the day. Most of the time you will be working with this person first when you arrive on set. There will be lots of time to get to know the person while they are working on you. Believe me; I have met some really cool people while sitting in that chair. This is your time before the shoot to relax and get in the swing of things for the day. Grab a coffee and enjoy. Makeup will be working pretty close to the set all day. Stepping in and out, touching things up when needed with powder and a variety of top secret gadgets.

Hair stylists will always be on set to turn whatever mop you show up with into a masterpiece. I am always surprised by the creations these people come up with. From a head full of pins holding up a James Dean do, to a hairspray helmet looking like a "Jetson" of the future.

All these people come together from all corners of the world to get the job done in the most efficient way possible. Learn your role in this equation early on and keep your feet on the ground. A professional photo set should run like a well oiled machine. Lots of high quality components coming together to do the best job they can within a given period of time and a set budget - it only takes one of the parts running a little off to make the day seem like it's dragging on and throw everything off. Wasted time means wasted money. Help the client to get the images they are looking to get as quickly as possible and they will re-book you. Throw a kink in things by being unprofessional or rude and you will never hear from them again.

Chapter 6: Authentic Modeling, Please Stop Posing

Have you ever looked at a beautiful picture and really asked yourself, "Why do I consider this picture exceptional? What about it is so captivating?" A well executed and composed photograph can move the soul. The fact is you can take a legendary photographer, for example Mario Testino; put a shy, inexperienced model on set and the pictures will come out mediocre at best. It is the photographer's job to compose and light the image, but as a model, you must bring your personality to the set. Stepping in front of the camera and becoming very self conscious or overly nervous is the worst possible thing you can do. Don't get me wrong, it is completely natural to be a little anxious in the beginning but, you can learn to control it. Through visualization techniques you can learn to reduce all your anxiety and use it to create the best possible outcome for the shoot. Believe me, being

on set in front of fifty complete strangers, either kissing a
pretty girl or trying to look comfortable in very little clothing
can make you ask certain questions of yourself. The
important thing to remember is that no matter what, they
chose you for this job. You would not be there on set if they
did not think that you were absolutely fitting for the image
they are trying to associate with their product. Reminding
yourself of this fact, quietly in your internal self talk, should
help to always keep a healthy perspective close at hand.

One of the things I also made a habit of doing early on, was
getting with the photographer before the first photo is
snapped and quickly discussing what the overall emotional
tone of the shoot was envisioned as being. Most of the time
the photographer will be glad that you cared enough to
understand the motivations before hand and will gladly
share with you any direction they can offer. Bottom line,
campaign and catalog modeling is about trying to sell
products. Models are some of the most exotic, sexy,
confident people in the world. The objective is simple, make
people think that, if they buy the product, they will attain
that sex appeal and become happier and more successful
themselves. So, to accomplish this goal you must always
imagine yourself as possessing those qualities.

Even if you are the clumsiest, most out of touch person in
the world, make it your mission to become this ideal the
second your foot hits the studio floor. Ask yourself: How
would a successful model be breathing? How would a

successful model be standing and walking? What would the internal self talk of a supermodel be? How would a super successful model be carrying their body? In my opinion, very upright and self assured, confident that they can accomplish the task at hand. Always ask yourself these questions before stepping on set. If, for some reason, you are being called to set and feel that your confidence is waning, ask for a couple of minutes, get in a quiet place, and begin the routine of changing your state of mind.

There are three key elements to changing your state of mind to that of a positive confident nature: posture (the way you carry your body), breathing and visualization, and maintaining a positive internal dialogue. You must completely believe that you are that sexy, confident and collected model in order to truly perform consistently at a professional level.

The working environment of a model is always changing. The people, the place, the language, the food, everything changes from job to job. There is no warming up period. You have to be ready to jump in to the deep end and completely go for it if you really want to be successful. If you find your sense of confidence faltering while on set always come back to the internal positive self talk of a top model, the focused breathing of a top model, carrying your body the way a confident top model would, and seeing yourself in your mind's eye as this totally successful top model by using visualization techniques. Remember, it is this positive self image and dynamic self-confidence that will come through on film and keep the clients calling. Put a piece of your personality, your humanity, in the picture and don't worry about what the masses are going to think of it, they will use it however they best see fit. There are people out there that will be touched by that little part of yourself they are able to sense, that sensibility and self confidence. Even if in the smallest way. Stay in the moment on set and above all, enjoy yourself. Remember, you are not saving the world, only making pretty pictures. The shots that are remembered are the ones able to connect on some other mysterious level and it always start with authentic models. It is our job to facilitate this emotion, this fantasy, by giving that energy to the camera.

Adjectives are also a very good way to get yourself going emotionally if you are asked to convey a specific energy or action. Modeling is basically a very simplistic form of acting. Actors will not appreciate that statement but, it is true. Instead of becoming the character for an entire scene, you become simple characters for a single frame at a time. You dress up in expensive clothing and waltz around expensive homes and luxurious locations and you live an alternate existence sometimes complete with a dog and a wife. Have fun with the fantasy of it all and allow yourself to live in the situation and the circumstances laid out by the photographer or create your own. Whatever you need to do in order to stay out of your own head.

While we are on the topic, I would like to address the idea of practicing poses and trying to emulate certain looks you might have seen in a campaign or magazine. In my opinion, poses are a really bad idea. No one wants to see you posing. It is an awkward thing to do and most models end up looking very awkward. Posing will not get you anywhere. Even when the photographer asks you to be still in a certain position, you must appear active. You must be focusing on something else so as to not appear you are being photographed at all. Models who are posing for the camera will only get to a certain level in the industry. The ones who have a sense of privacy when being photographed are the ones who ultimately create quality images the larger clients are willing to pay good money for. These unguarded, private images are the reason models get paid.

Chapter 7: Runway Modeling During Fashion Week

Fashion week is, hands down, the most important week of the year for models in the high fashion industry. Designers, buyers, agents, models, photographers, all gather in the fashion capitals, New York, Paris, Milano, to see what the latest styles are for the upcoming season. In this chapter we will focus primarily on the role of the model during this week and what fashion week represents for the individual's career path.

Milano is the first of the fashion capitals to show. Then comes Paris directly following with their own show season, complete with different designers. After that, it's back to the states to wrap it all up in New York City. All the models arrive about a week before the shows in Milan, through Malpensa or Linate airports, and begin to make the rounds of castings for the shows. Show casting are your chance to meet all of the top designers in the world face to face, Dolce & Gabbana, Calvin Klein, Gucci, Fendi, Prada, along with many others, all of them big names that can either make or break your career. Be prepared to do a lot of walking around and a lot of changing clothes and waiting around.

The week of castings can be very hectic and downright chaotic at times; it's not out of the norm for a model to literally run to 10 castings in a day during fashion week. Take my advice, partner up with a few other models from your agency and rent a car and driver for the week. One show will pay for the cost and you will save yourself a lot of time and headache. I know that doesn't sound like a lot right now but, just wait until casting number seven rolls around and your feet ache, it's hot, and you still have not had the chance to eat anything all day.

Show castings are much different than a catalog or editorial casting. Most of the time show castings are absolutely flooded with models and can take a while to get through each one. Make sure that you have something to keep your mind occupied otherwise; you end up just standing there for a couple hours staring at nothing, either freezing or sweating. I have seen there be as few as two or three to as many as two hundred models all lined up ready to walk for the designers and their team. The design houses have been better recently about picking the models they see as potentially walking in the show before hand and only requesting the models they know fit their collection's criteria, which is nice because it really helps to speed up the day for everyone.

When you go into a runway casting it is important for you to have excellent posture. Posture really does matter when you are auditioning for these jobs, not so much any other time in the industry but, in this instance, the designers are definitely going for a certain look and body type and they will very seldom sway from their criteria. As soon as you walk in, a casting team will be sitting at a table waiting to look at your book and have you walk. By walk, I mean they will have you walk as if you were on the runway in an actual show, usually a short jaunt down the hall or across the room will suffice.

If you begin to feel self-conscious and question yourself at this point it is important to go back to your focused breathing, internal self-talk, and the way you carry your body. Remember, breathing, positive internal self talk, and the way you carry your body, when they are all used together have a profound effect on your internal mental state and the overall way that your presence comes across during your castings, on the runway, or on set. Use these tools to help you maintain your poise and confidence.

Many times there will be a large number of people in the room. After you have walked, the casting team will decide if they think that you fit the overall image of their clothing line. If you do, you will be asked to try on some of the clothes that will most likely be displayed in the shows and then a Polaroid shot will be taken and stapled to your card. This is pretty much the status quo for a fashion week casting.

At the end of each day you will call in to your agency, check to see what the castings are looking like for the next day and which designers are holding options on you for their shows. Most of the time the agency will have your schedule for the next day faxed to the hotel the night before and you will receive it either that night, or the next morning on your way out.

The next step in the casting process is the fitting. If the designer decides that you have the right image for their product and that it is a good possibility you will do the show, they will call the agency to request a fitting. This does not necessarily mean that you have the job but, you are one step closer. Most of the time the fittings are held at the fashion house headquarters. At the fitting you will work first hand with the designers as they hand pick a selection of clothing from their new collection you will be modeling in the show. Fittings generally go pretty quickly but, sometimes they can take a while depending on the designer, the number of models who are there for a fitting as well, and how many outfits, or looks, you have for the show.

After the clothes have been pinned and tailored to fit you, you will walk, once again, to give the design team an idea of what the outfit looks like on you in motion. Further adjustments will be made. Clothing will be added and taken away until the designer and stylist are satisfied with the look. A Polaroid will be taken to document what clothing you were wearing and will also be helpful to your dresser when they are trying to get an idea of what your outfit should look like before the actual runway show. Just because you go through the fitting process does not mean that you will be confirmed for the show. However, it is considered quite rare to go through a fitting process and not be confirmed for the actual show. Most of the time you will know before you leave the fitting if you are going to be walking in the show.

Just like any other job, before the show you will be sent a call time and the details of location and rate. Designers often prefer for you to arrive at least three hours before the show is scheduled to start. Clients will allow models to be late during fashion week if they are doing another show with a minor scheduling conflict. However, this is the exception to the rule, not the norm. Best policy is to be on time. Remember, this is your chance to leave the best possible impression of yourself on the design house. The extra time before the show also allows you to chill out, get something to eat, go through the hair and makeup process, and any required rehearsals to prepare for the show. Expect to spend a good amount of time waiting. It is best to take something to keep yourself occupied in a constructive manner.

About an hour before the show you will be called to the runway to go through a quick rehearsal of how everyone will enter and exit the runway and any other requests the designer and producer of the show may have. Pay attention and you will be fine. It is far from rocket science. All you have to remember is where to enter, where to stop once you are out on the runway, and where to exit the runway. If you don't pay attention, you end up being that person that comes out from backstage, does something ridiculously out of sync, and ruins the show. If for some reason you get out on the runway and find yourself lost, don't panic, just look at what the person is doing in front of you and breathe. Believe me, fashion shows are really hard to screw up. Ladies, of course, have it a little harder with some of the heels and the catwalk strut required of female models. This is a very specific style of walking the runway which we will discuss in detail later on.

Backstage, all the models will begin to get dressed in their first looks for the show around thirty minutes prior to the music and lights being cued. Backstage is usually just a really large room resembling a walk-in closet. People will be sleeping, eating, talking, reading, getting hair and makeup done. Big shows especially, can be mad houses. All the clothes will be tailored and hung on racks waiting for the models. Your composite card will be hanging next to your outfits, or looks, for the show, find it when you arrive and know where it is in order to avoid any last minute panic when the producer calls you to get dressed for the show. Standing next to your area should be your dresser, a person that will be assisting you in all the fast changes you will need to make throughout the duration of the show.

Fashion shows are not for the faint of heart. As the start of the show draws near, the choreographer will begin to organize the models into a line in the order you will be walking out on to the runway. This is when things start to get interesting. The entire process starts out very slow and bland and ends in a frenzied spectacle. From backstage you can sense the crowd growing and can feel the anticipation build. If a live band is performing, they are getting warmed up. Blood running hot, the countdown begins. The designers do one last run through the line to make sure everyone is looking just the way they intend. The place goes dark, the crowd gets quiet and for a moment there is silence. Tension fills the air as everyone awaits the first beat of the music and Boom! The lights burst on in perfect sync with the music and the show has started. From backstage you can feel the bass of the speakers as it replaces the beat of your heart. A choreographer will be at the front of the line timing the release of the models onto the runway. Once it is your turn to make your entrance, take a deep breath, remember that you are not saving the world, and have a good time with it.

It is a good idea to never focus on one face in the crowd for too long. In fact, you are better off trying to pretend the crowd is not there at all. You are just taking a super confident stroll through the park. If you engage the audience in more than a passing way, it ruins the pace and slight illusion of the show. Let your steps fall in with the beat of the music. The tempo will usually inform you of the pace intended for the show. When you come to the end of the runway, you will encounter the largest wall of photographers you have ever seen. Be cool. Hopefully, you were told in rehearsal exactly what kind of movement is expected of you in this moment. If you weren't, not a big deal, just take a quick moment to pause for the cameras and give them a chance to photograph the outfit you are wearing from a couple of angles. Then, just turn around and walk down the other side. Piece of cake.

Every runway show strives to be highly energetic, fun, exciting and memorable. Your mentality during the walk should be no different than it is when you find yourself on a photo shoot. Be what you are, young, sexy, and confident. Hopefully, well dressed. After the first go around you rush back stage to your dresser. Believe me, this is the fastest you will ever see a group of people change clothes. You should focus on getting undressed while your dresser is focused on dressing. In order to change clothes in time to get back on stage quickly you need to be taking off your shirt and shoes as you are approaching your dressing station. Work with your dresser as a team and you should be fine. After all it is just changing clothes, albeit ten times faster than you normally change. As you are transforming into your second look of the night, the choreographer is screaming your name, you are next. Once again, hit the runway in stride, rinse, and repeat. Like I said, pay attention during the rehearsal and you will be golden.

The show ends and everyone is backstage in a big circle clapping and thanking each other, hugging, and celebrating a job well done. These moments are the ones worth sticking it out for, special moments that you will carry with you for the rest of your life. For a few moments, a room full of strangers becomes a team and creates this odd spectacle and somehow it all works. Everything in modeling is a team effort; no part exists completely separate from the other. So much work goes into this week from so many angles but, it is all worth the effort when you feel the rush of adrenaline and have the sense of accomplishment that comes with a job well done.

Most fashion shows are followed by an after party and if you do the show you will be invited. If you didn't do the show, don't sweat it, there is usually someone staying in your hotel that did the show and can get you in. If this is not the case, ask your agent if they can get you in. Sometimes it is a good idea to go to parties during fashion week simply to network and meet new people in the industry. Although it is important to have fun at the parties during fashion week, keep in mind, you are always at work. You are a professional amongst professionals. Most everyone at the parties will be connected to the business in some way or another. So, don't get trashed and start crying about your ex-lover or being generally out of hand, you could end up hurting your career and have a bad headache in the morning to boot. Look at parties as your chance to meet people and network with industry players. I am not suggesting you stalk the designer or anyone else but it doesn't hurt to attend the after party and politely congratulate and thank them for hiring you to walk in the show.

Chapter 8: Potential Modeling Markets

Modeling markets exist all over the world. In order to consistently work as a model, you will need to establish a network of agencies and clients spanning numerous continents. This is not as hard as it sounds. A good agency can help you establish most of these connections and the agency submission process I have previously described works well with foreign agencies too.

Fashion week is a great opportunity to meet agents from all of these markets as most of them will be in attendance. Modeling agencies exist all over the world in most cities with any economy to speak of. However, in this book, the focus is on the major markets of London, Paris, New York, Milan, Germany, Sweden, Spain, South Africa, Japan, and

Brazil, where models are most likely to make the most money and have the most access to a solid base of editorial, catalog, and campaign clients.

Chapter 9: Different Categories of Bookings and What to Expect

In the industry there are four different categories that a photo shoot booking will likely fall under. There are photo tests, editorials, catalog, and campaigns. All equally important but, very different in the end result and most importantly, financial gain. By this I mean booking certain jobs can help you build your portfolio and bring the exposure needed to be considered for bigger jobs but won't necessarily be financially rewarding and sometimes vice versa.

It is important to always keep the bigger vision of the direction you see your career going in mind when choosing which jobs you decide to do. Be aware of what specific clients and magazines represent in the scheme of the modeling industry and how you will be perceived should you choose to work for them. For example, once you reach a certain level of the industry, you don't want to accidentally shoot yourself in the foot by doing some cheesy work for Wal-Mart or a similar client. The larger fashion houses and beauty clients will see this and immediately disassociate themselves from you. It's just the name of the game. However, if you are only modeling part time and looking to earn some extra money, by all means, take every job that comes along and get it while the getting is good. Don't worry, a good modeling agent will know all of this very well and can help you navigate your way to a consistent career.

Most of the time a new model will start a career with only a few pictures in their book from recent test shoots. This is a perfectly valid way to get started and your agency will most likely facilitate this process. In the beginning, be prepared to basically work for free, or next to free, until you get enough tears from editorial work in your book to be considered for larger, higher paying jobs. When you only have a few pictures to display the trick is to choose only the photos you believe are the strongest. Otherwise you will end up insecure while you are on castings with prospective clients and that is extremely detrimental to your chances of being cast. Trust your instinct on this one and you will be fine. Ask yourself which shots best represent you and the image that you believe you want to convey to clients within the industry.

Most of the time, particularly in the beginning, your agent will arrange your book the best way they see fit. Trust them but, don't be afraid to assert yourself and voice your opinion. Remember, it is your career and you are ultimately the one who has to go out and present this book to clients. It is better to have four really strong images in a book than to have twenty mediocre shots that leave the client feeling nothing.

Early in your career will most likely be about trying to book shoots for editorials. Editorials are the pictures that comprise the spreads you see in the fashion magazines such as Vogue, W, Arena Hommes+, and I.D. Editorials shot with credible photographers will allow you to take your book to a completely different level through the use of what we call "tears". Tear sheet is just another name for the pictures you literally tear out of the magazine it is featured in and place in your book. The more good tears you have in your book, the better. Quality tears let the client know that if they spend thousands of dollars on your day rate, fly you in for a job, and put you up in a hotel, it won't be a waste. Bottom line, editorials help to give you the experience you need to perform at higher levels and develop a book that will keep the clients coming back for the long haul.

Appearing in high profile campaigns are obviously the best tears you can have in the book when in the casting process for jobs. Campaigns in the book say to the clients and other photographers that you can handle yourself on the most professional of sets where big budgets are on the line. When selecting faces for jobs, clients will always look to the models that have been in major ad campaigns before any other models are considered. However, there is some confusion regarding the rates models can expect to get paid for a high profile campaign. Often times, unless the model is a recognizable face or a celebrity of some sort, they can expect to make about the same money they would on a catalog shoot. Yes, they pay better than editorials and shows but, don't expect to retire off one campaign or two or three for that matter. One of the reasons major campaigns don't pay much is they know you will book other jobs from the tears, and the exposure you get from booking high profile jobs is priceless, which is a fair trade, sort of. Either way, it's the way it is, so get used to it.

Fragrances and beauty contracts are a completely different class of booking. Perfume, hair and makeup lines generate major income for corporations, allowing for an increased rate for the model. Book a major fragrance or skincare ad and depending on the buyout or usage, you could potentially be looking at a considerable amount of money. These types of jobs are what high fashion modeling careers are always striving to attain. Lancôme, Maybelline, Estee Lauder are good examples of the clients usually offering this type of booking opportunity.

As previously discussed, fashion week plays a major role in the exposure aspect of your career. Runways are the single most concentrated medium of exposure a model can hope for beyond high profile fragrances and ad campaigns. Every person who has anything to do with fashion will attend the bigger runway shows. Runways are your chance to get in front of all the clients in concentrated bursts. Fashion week also gives you the opportunity to pass out your composite card and start circulating your image within the business. Even if you don't think that your look is right for the particular show, go to the casting and make certain that the casting director or designer has your composite card.

All this work building your book is ultimately done to get the fragrance and beauty contracts but the bread and butter jobs of the industry are catalog. Catalogs are the only clients that have enough money and business to keep your pockets lined. Once you have done the work establishing yourself in the runway, editorial, and ad campaigns you will be able to charge the catalog clients a higher day rate. Granted, the other jobs will often be more interesting, but at the end of the day, we are still in the business to make money. Big companies like Bloomingdale's, Macy's, and Saks Fifth Avenue have the money to pay top models their high day rates and the volume of business to consistently book them. In fact, these are the only clients that are willing to book you frequently enough to establish any sort of reliable income in this industry. The only thing to remember is - you are selling the clothes. The clothes should always be considered number one priority on this particular type of job. Look forward to long days without much of a break. It is not out of the ordinary for models to shoot 40 different looks for a catalog day. This high number of shots is the new normal.

Sometimes you might get lucky and land a job with a catalog client in a great location shooting a "book" for a holiday or special sale but, generally you will be in a studio on a closed set for ten hours. Not a bad thing, but just the way it is when it comes to catalog jobs these days.

Eventually you will reach a point in your career where you have created a base of clients who book you frequently enough that you begin to establish a reliable monthly income from which to operate. On the way to this level of financial security things can get a little stressful at times. No matter how successful you are, there is always the question of when, and if, that next job will present itself to you. In reality, models are independent contractors always looking for the next job to fill the pipeline and finances tend to fluctuate month to month. Not to be discouraging but, if you book a great editorial or a big campaign it does not guarantee that you will be successful in the long run. Models are constantly employed and immediately unemployed following the wrap of the shoot. This does not mean that you cannot make a substantial income; it just means that you are always looking for work so save your money. Remain balanced and consistently professional and you will exponentially increase your odds of success.

Chapter 10: Avoiding Scams

Unfortunately, there are people out there that pose as knowledgeable representatives within the industry, people that own bogus modeling schools and talent agencies who will not think twice about taking money and valuable time away from starry eyed young men and women looking for a way to break in to the industry. The best way to avoid being a victim of these pitfalls is awareness of some of the scams that you can fall into. Protect yourself with knowledge early on and it will be a lot harder for people to take advantage of you. I am not suggesting that you turn into a paranoid cynic, just watch yourself. Credible agents will put their money where their mouth is and you will soon see progress with your career. Hacks will ultimately reveal themselves over time by not being able to back any of the promises that they have made. Sit back, take your time, and do your homework. This is your career and you are the one ultimately responsible for protecting your best interest at the end of the day.

Many models, upon first starting out in the business tend to think that there is some sort of educational background or specialized model training that can somehow put them ahead of the curve. Often times these courses and modeling conventions can cost thousands of dollars with little or no return on your investment. Granted it is possible to meet an agent willing to sign you at a talent search but it is completely unnecessary. All that is required before entering the industry is that have a unique or classic look you can display comfortably and naturally in front of a camera. Too many naïve models get roped into paying thousands of dollars for bogus courses in modeling or test shoot preparation. Often times, the people teaching these high priced courses are not at all qualified. They have never been on a set or around the real modeling industry in any way. They will tell you things to make you believe they are important and connected but it is often a facade. Once you get an agent, it is part of their job to teach you everything you need to know about the business. This stuff is not rocket science; don't make it more complicated than it is.

Modeling conventions are held by large companies that enable aspiring models to meet with agents face to face. However, they are expensive and the process resembles a cattle auction. You will be outfitted in all the same colors, black or white, and given numbers as identifiers. After this you will be asked to walk on a stage in a mock runway show in front of a panel of agents and scouts. Now, I am not saying that this is an illegitimate business practice. However, it is probably the most expensive way to go about breaking into the industry. Save yourself some time and money and put the work into sending out your information and pictures to all the agencies you are interested in working with.

Another area of caution is shooting nude photography. When nude pictures are shot with class and style they can turn out really nice and be a solid addition to a book. It is best policy in these situations to use your instincts. As long as you are working with someone you trust and it has been predetermined the photo shoot will be nude or it fits with overall theme of the story, I say go for it. However, if you are working with a photographer you don't know well and they start to suggest losing the clothes and inappropriate poses, you might want to rethink the situation. This goes double if you are on an editorial shoot for a magazine that will be distributed all over the country or better yet, the world. End up in a spread wearing nothing but your birthday suit and it could serve to really embarrass, not only you, but the agency as well and you might just find yourself without an agency when it is all said and done.

Beware of any agency that sells modeling packages or requires you pay them a fee to represent you. Shady agencies are set up to make money directly from the models and not the commissions made from booking models quality work. Reputable agencies will make their money from the commission they make from the jobs they help you to book. Shady agencies will have a network of people that they are used to working with, everyone from photographers, printing companies, to modeling schools. Everyone takes a cut and you are left with nothing but a lighter wallet. These agencies even employ scouts to keep a fresh crop of models running through the network. By the time it is all over with, you have spent potentially thousands of dollars and made little to no progress with your career.

I myself have had bad experiences early on in my career by paying a no name agency to represent me. Every time that I would call to check in, my "agent" would be in a meeting or out to lunch, always unavailable. When I would manage to get in touch he would always say in a sleazy accent, "RC, where have you been? I've been trying to get a hold of you for weeks." Yeah, I'm sure. Always do your homework and make sure the agency you are signing with is legitimate and has a solid track record. Ignore this advice and find yourself out of a few thousand bucks, a lot of time, and very discouraged. Be aware of what can occur and you will not be a victim of these unethical business practices.

Chapter 11: Modeling as a Stepping Stone

Modeling can be a long term career for some and will be a stepping stone for others. Either way, you will have a lot of down time both on set and off in between jobs. You can potentially make enough money if your cards are played carefully, to give you a great head start in life. An important realization in modeling is being able to cope with the fact that, for most people, this is a temporary lifestyle. Even supermodels have a career span. Top models often find themselves branching off into other facets of business later on when nature inevitably has its way. It is important early on in your career to remember that, although you might not have control over the amount of work you get, or the span of your career, you do have complete control over how productively you spend your free time and the money that you are able to make, especially if you are living in a major city. Pay attention when you are on set. There are so many avenues to explore as you will come into contact with people from all over the world who are walking down very different career paths. There will be many opportunities for you to expand and determine what comes next.

Models are able to make large sums of cash relatively quickly. What you decide to do with this cash now could dramatically affect your life in the future. A lot of younger models book a couple of big jobs, make some decent cash, and head straight to the clubs and department stores. Now, don't get me wrong, while it is important to always remind yourself of why you are working, you have to be smart about it. You can set yourself up to look the part with expensive clothes and bottles of expensive alcohol but, you are only playing a part. In the morning you will wake up with a bad head ache and empty pockets. By living within your means, or a little below, you allow a good portion of your money to be utilized for the future. Modeling does not have a pension plan, insurance, paid vacation, or a 401K. All of these are left up to you to establish for your own good using the money you have earned. Keep in mind, we are self employed and depend on working with agencies to find new modeling jobs.

Another thing to consider during your down time is some sort of secondary education. College courses are now offered online and can be attended from almost anywhere in the world according to your schedule and educational needs. Acting is also another valid avenue that models should consider. Many of the successful actors and actresses you see on the big screen today were once models themselves. There is no better place than New York City to study acting either. Some of the best acting coaches and companies are located within the city.

Avoid this type of regret and invest your money in worthwhile, educated ventures while the money is rolling in. A financial planner can help you use the money that you have earned to make more money through a sound investment strategy. A lot of successful models go into real estate or start their own businesses. These are the investments that will generate the financial cushion that will allow you to transition into other career avenues when your career in modeling comes to a close.

Bottom line, modeling will allow you to make good money for a period of time but the nature of the industry is change. New faces quickly come and go. Granted there are established faces within the industry that never seem to age or fade out. If this is you, kudos my friend. You are one of the lucky few. While you are hot, things are rocking and you are living the life. Do yourself a favor and be smart with your time and money from the start. This is the only way that you won't look back later on and think, "what if?"

Chapter 12: Networking and Self Promotion as a Model

Most of the promotional responsibilities in your career will fall upon the shoulders of your agent. It is their job to make sure clients know you exist in whatever way they can. Usually this is accomplished through what is called a "mailer" and good old fashioned picking up the phone and spreading the news. Mailers are basically packages of your image and information that are digitally sent out to the network of clients and other agencies across the globe the agency works with. Agencies have relationships with other agencies and help each other find new talent. If an agency in New York City finds a fresh face with potential; they will usually help that person find representation in other markets with agencies they are accustomed to working with.

With that said, there are a few things you can do on your own to potentially pick up new clients and help build your career faster and more efficiently. Let's take a look below.

The internet and social media have really changed the game for models. It allows you to be more pro-active and get your face out there across the globe without ever leaving your home. If you are booked on a high profile campaign that comes along with a lot of exposure, people are going to need a place to find information about you and your career. Hiring someone to build or, better yet, building your own personal website is a really good idea. It gives the appearance you have already attained a certain level of success in the industry even if you are just starting out. It can be done relatively cheaply these days and the benefits far outweigh the costs. Make certain the site has its own blog as well and occasionally make a post about your thoughts on fashion or share some of your experiences traveling and working on sets.

Over time you will develop a presence on the web and the search engines will start to direct traffic to your site. The internet is such an amazing invention and we are just starting to tap into its potential for making connection and networking. You never know who could randomly stumble across your site and decide your face is exactly what they are looking for. Could be a new photographer offering to photograph you for free or it could be the president of Lancôme looking for a new face to represent a skincare product. Point is, you never know. Also, if you dedicate a bit of time to building the traffic of your site through blog posts and linking strategies, you can attach Google AdSense and other advertisements turning it into a passive revenue generator for yourself. That's another book though.

Establishing a Twitter and Facebook account for yourself as a model is also important in this day and age. Many, many clients and casting directors have accounts of their own which makes it easier than ever before to get your face in front of them. Having a healthy number of followers on Twitter and fans established through social media networks is never a bad idea. Not all clients will care but, more and more these days having a presence on the web and being able to prove you have access to a fair amount of people is considered a commodity. It is very valuable to be able to say that if they book you for a campaign, people will undoubtedly care. Having followers is a good way to prove that.

Throughout your career you will be presented with opportunities to attend parties and other fashion related social gatherings. These are always a good idea to attend, particularly in the beginning when you are trying to establish yourself in the industry. Even if you only go for a little while and say hello, it will still give people a chance to see your face and possibly get to know you a bit. Again, composure is key. Successful models always carry themselves with a sense of style and grace. Be whoever you want to be at home, even wear pajamas all day, it doesn't matter but, when you are out with the industry crowd, it is very important to look your best. Yes, it is a party but, you are at work. I am not suggesting you bring your book along or comp cards but just know people that matter are most likely watching and will remember you for better or worse.

Departure

Now my friend, you have armed yourself with knowledge. Even having prepared yourself, know that you are about to go on an unpredictable adventure. Who knows where you might end up? To me, that is the beauty of this ride. While, just like everything else, with the good comes the bad, the adventure is still worth being undertaken. Travel and meet people. Learn to replace the arrogance with confidence.

You will learn things in your time in this business that you will never see in a book. Take pictures. Write it all down in a journal, someday, when this is all just a memory, you will look back and remember that period of time when you were young, traveling the world, learning all that you could about yourself.

Throughout your career you will experience tremendous highs and lows. The high times will seem surreal and the lows never ending. However, it is important to keep a relative perspective on what you are doing. There are very few people in the world that are able do and enjoy the journey that you are about to embark upon. Every once in a while take a step back from it all and really feel the uniqueness of your situation. Be it a moment to reflect on all the wonderful souls you've come in contact with or just to appreciate the skyline of whatever city you are in. This is the type of job that is here one moment and gone the next. Savor every ounce of it, make intelligent decisions and you will never look back with regrets. Good Luck!

Global Top Modeling Agencies List

New York City

DNA Model Management
555 West 25th St.6th fl
New York, NY 10001
Ph: 212 226 0080
Email: info@dnamodels.com
Web: dnamodels.com

Elite New York
245 Fifth Avenue, 24th Floor
New York, NY 10016
Ph: 212 529 9700
Web: elitemodel.com

Ford Models
111 Fifth Avenue
New York, NY 10003
Ph: 212 219 6500
Web: fordmodels.com

IMG Models
304 Park Avenue South, 12th Floor
New York, NY 10010
Ph: 212 253 8884
Web: imgmodels.com

Major Model Management
419 Park Avenue South, Suite #1201
New York, NY 10016
Ph: 212 685 1200
Email: info@majormodel.com
Web: majormodel.com

NEXT Models
15 Watts Street, 6th floor
New York, NY 10013
Ph: 212 925 5100
Web: nextmodels.com

New York Model Management
596 Broadway, 7th Floor
New York, NY 10012
Ph: 212 539 1700
Web: newyorkmodels.com

Marilyn Modeling Agency
24-32 Union Square East, PH
New York, NY 10003
Ph: 212 260 6500
Web: marilynagency.com

Wilhelmina Models 300 Park Avenue South
New York, NY 10010
Ph: 212 473 0700
Web: wilhelmina.com

One Management
42 Bond Street, 2nd Floor
New York, NY 10012
Ph: 212 505 5545
Email: info@onemanagement.com
Web: onemanagement.com

Supreme Management
199 Lafayette Street, 7th Floor
New York, NY 10012
Ph: 212 334 7480
Web: suprememanagement.com

Women Model Management
199 Lafayette Street, 7th Floor
New York, NY 10012
Ph: 212 334 7480
Web: womenmanagement.com

Request Models
36 East 20th, 7th Floor
New York, NY 10010 Ph: 212 529 4130
Email: info@requestmodels.com
Web: requestmodels.com

Soul Artist Management
11 West 25th Street, 9th Floor
New York, NY 10010
Ph: 646 827 1188
Email: info@soulartistmanagement.com
Web: soulartistmanagement.com

VNY Model Management
928 Broadway Suite 700
New York, NY 10010
Ph: 212 206 1012
Web: vnymodelmanagement.com

Los Angeles

LA Models
7700 Sunset Blvd
Los Angeles, CA
Ph: 323.436.7705
Web: lamodels.com

Ford Models
9200 Sunset Blvd.
West Hollywood, CA
Ph: 310.276.8100
Web: fordmodels.com

Nous Model Mgmt
117 North Robertson Blvd
Los Angeles, CA 90048
Ph: 310.385.6900
Web: nousmodels.com

Affinity Artists Agency
5724 w.3rd #511
Los Angeles, CA 90036
Ph: 323.525.0577
Web: affinityartists.com

Chicago

Chosen Management
58 W. Huron
Chicago, IL 60654
Ph: 312-274-1868
Web: chosenchicago.com

Aria Talent
1017 West Washington, Suite 2C
Chicago, IL 60607
Ph: 312.850.9671
Web: arlenewilson.com

Ford Models
1017 W Washington Blvd #2C
Chicago, IL 60607
Ph: 312 243-9400
Web: fordmodels.com

Elite Model Management
58 West Huron
Chicago, Illinois
Ph: 312.943.3226
Web: elitechicago.com / elitemodel.com

Dallas

Page 214 Model & Talent
3303 Lee Parkway #205
Dallas, TX 75219
Ph: 214.526.4434
Web: pageparkes.com

Kim Dawson Agency
1645 North Stemmons Freeway
Dallas, TX 75207
Ph: 214.638.2414
Web: kimdawsonagency.com

The Campbell Agency
3838 Oak Lawn Ave. #900
Dallas, TX 75219
Ph: 214.522.8991
Web: thecampbellagency.com

Dallas Model Group
12300 Ford Road #305
Dallas, TX 75230
Ph: 972.980.7647
Web: dmgmanagement.com

The Clutts Agency
1825 Market Center Blvd #380
Dallas, TX 75207
Ph: 214.761.1400
Web: thecluttsagency.com

Miami

Next Model Management
1688 Meridian Avenue #800
Miami Beach, FL
Ph: 305 531-5100

Elite Models
119 Washington Avenue #501
Miami Beach, FL
Ph: 305 674-9500

Wilhelmina Models
1100 West Avenue
Miami Beach, FL
Ph: 305 672-9344

Mega Models
420 Lincoln Road #408
Miami Beach, FL
Ph: 305 672-6342

Ford Models
1665 Washington Avenue
Miami Beach, FL Ph: 305 534-7200

Barcelona

Elite Barcelona
Country: Spain
Rambla Catalunya 81 4 2
Barcelona 08008
Ph: +34 93 272 09 09
Email: barcelona@elitemodel.es
Web: elitemodel.es

Sight Management Studio
Country: Spain
Paseo de Gracia 37 2 2
Barcelona 08007
Ph: +34 93 272 24 34
Email: scouting@sight-management.com
Web: sight-management.com

Traffic Models
Country: Spain
Pasaje Sert, 2
Barcelona 08010
Ph: +34 93 41 4 02 68
Email: models@trafficmodels.com
Web: trafficmodels.com

Uno Models
Country: Spain
Av Marquès de l'Argentera 5
Barcelona 08003
Ph: +34 93 444 43 02
Web: unobcn.com

View Management
Country: Spain
Paseo de Gracia, 601 C
Barcelona 08007
Ph: +34 93 272 09 99
Email: scoutwomen@viewmanagement.com
Web: viewmanagement.com

London

Elite London
Country: United Kingdom
3-5 Islington High Street
London N1 9LQ
Ph: +44 (0) 20 7841 3288
Email: info@elitemodellondon.co.uk
Web: elitemodellondon.co.uk

IMG London
Country: United Kingdom
8 Flitcroft Street
London WC2H8DJ
Ph: +44 20 8233 6770
Web: imgmodels.com

Models 1
Country: United Kingdom
12 Macklin Street Covent Garden
London WC2B 5SZ
Ph: +44 0 20 7025 4900
Email: info@models1.co.uk
Web: models1.co.uk

NEXT London
Country: United Kingdom
Ground Floor, Blocks B & C, Morelands Buildings
5-23 Old Street
London EC1V 9HL
Ph: +44 207 251 9850
Web: nextmodels.com

Premiere Model Management
Country: United Kingdom 40-42 Parker Street
London WC2B 5PQ
Ph: +44 0 20 7333 0888
Email: info@PremierModelManagement.com
Web: premiermodelmanagement.com

Select Model Management
Country: United Kingdom
27 Mortimer Street
London W1T 3JG
Ph: +44 207 299 1355
Email: women@selectmodel.com
men@selectmodel.com
Web: selectmodel.com

Storm Model Management
Country: United Kingdom
5 Jubilee Place
London SW3 3TD
Ph: +44 207 368 9967
Email: info@stormmodels.co.uk
Web: stormmodels.com

Tess Management
Country: United Kingdom
9-10 Market Place 4th floor
London W1W 8AQ
Ph: +44 20 7557 7100
Web: tessmanagement.com

Viva London
Country: United Kingdom
23 Charlotte Road, 3rd Floor
London EC2A 3PB
Ph: +44 203 487 1240
Web: viva-paris.com

Paris

Elite Models
Country: France
19 Avenue George V
Paris 75008
Ph: +33 1 40 44 32 22
Web: elitemodel.fr

Ford Models Europe
Country: France
3 Rue de Choiseul
Paris 75002
Ph: +33 1 53 05 25 25
Web: fordmodelseurope.com

IMG Paris
Country: France
8 Rue Danielle Casanova
Paris 75002
Ph: +33 1 55 35 12 00
Web: imgmodels.com

Major Paris
Country: France
14 Rue Favart
Paris 75002
Ph: +33 0 1 40 20 15 15
Email: info@majorparis.fr
Web: majorparis.fr

Marilyn Agency
Country: France
4, Rue de la Paix
Paris 75002
Ph: +33 1 53 29 53 53
Web: marilynagency.com

Nathalie Models
Country: France
6 Rue de Braque
Paris 75003
Ph: +33 1 44 29 07 10
Web: nathalie-models.com

NEXT Paris
Country: France
9 Boulevard de La Madeleine
Paris 75001
Ph: +33 1 5345 1300
Web: nextmodels.com

Oui Management
Country: France
20 Passage Dauphine
Paris 75006
Ph: +33 1 4326 3232
Web: ouimanagement.com

Silent Models
Country: France
54 Rue Ponthieu
Paris 75008
Ph: +33 1 780 954 40
Email: info@silentmodels.com
Web: silentmodels.com

Viva Model Management
Country: France
15 Rue Duphot
Paris 75001
Ph: +33 1 44 55 12 60
Email: info@viva-paris.com
Web: viva-paris.com

Women Paris
Country: France
7 Bd de La Madeleine
Paris 75001
Ph: +33 1 55 35 22 22
Web: womenmanagement.fr

Angels & Demons
Country: France
34 Rue du Faubourg Saint Honore
Paris 75008
Ph: +33 (0)1 42 68 24 44
Email: info@angels-models.com
Web: angels-models.com

Success Models
Country: France
11-13 Rue des Arquesbusiers
Paris 75003
Ph: +33 0 1 42 78 89 89
Email: liana@successmodels.com
Web: successmodels.com

Hamburg

Iconic Management
Country: Germany
Hohe Bleichen 13
Hamburg 20354
Ph: +49 40 2788 20260
Web: iconicmanagement.com

M4 Models
Country: Germany
79 Rothenbaumchaussee
Hamburg 20148
Ph: +49 40 413 2360
Email: Hamburg@m4models.de
Web: m4models.de

MD Management
Country: Germany
Eppendorfer Weg 213
Hamburg 20253
Ph: +49 40 42 10 76 660
Email: info@md-management.com
Web: md-management.com

Mega Model Agency
Country: Germany
Kaiser-Wilhelm-Strasse
93 Hamburg D-20355
Ph: +49 0 40 355 2200
Web: megamodelagency.com

Model Management
Country: Germany
Hartungstrasses 5
Hamburg 20146
Ph: +49 40 44 05 55
Email: alexandra@model-management.de
Web: model-management.de

Modelwerk
Country: Germany
Rothenbaumchaussee 1
Hamburg 20149
Ph: +49 40 88 30 73 - 0
Email: booker@modelwerk.de
Web: modelwerk.de

Place Models
Country: Germany
Am Felde 29
Hamburg 22765
Ph: +49 (0) 40 460 79 60
Email: info@placemodels.com
Web: placemodels.com

Spin Model Management
Country: Germany
Ferdinand-Beit-Strasse 7b
Hamburg 20099
Ph: +49 40 7296-8000
Email: Info@spinmodelmanagement.com
Web: spinmodelmanagement.com

Stockholm

Elite Stockholm
Country: Sweden
Grev Turegatan 18
Stockholm 114 46
Ph: +46 854 586 666
Email: info@elitemodel.se
Web: elitemodel.se

Mikas
Country: Sweden
Bredgrand 2
Stockholm 11130
Ph: +46 8 57 88 00 00
Email: johan@mikas.se
Web: mikas.se

Modellink
Country: Sweden
Magasinsgatan 10
Stockholm 411 18
Ph: +46 31 13 15 33
Email: info@modellink.se
Web: modellink.se

Tokyo

Bon Image Group
Country: Japan
1-15-14-8 Minamiaoyama Minato-ku
Tokyo 107-0062
Ph: +81 3 3403 4110
Email: info@image-tokyo.co.jp
Web: image-tokyo.co.jp

Bravo Models
Country: Japan
Hillside Terrace H-301, 18-17 Sarugakuch
Shibuya-ku
Tokyo 150-0033
Ph: +81 3 3463 9090
Email: bravo.scouting@q.com
Web: bravomodels.net

Donna Models
Country: Japan
Jinnan Plaza #603 1.15.3 Jinnan Shibuya-ku
Tokyo 150-0041
Ph: +81 03 3770 8255
Email: info@donnamodels.jp
Web: donnamodels.jp

Zucca Model Agency
Country: Japan
Towa Komaba Co-op #303 2-18-5 Tomigaya Shibuya-ku
Tokyo 151-0063
Ph: +81 3 3465 5851
Email: info@zucca-models.co.jp
Web: zucca-models.co.jp

Sydney

Chic Management
Country: Australia
36 Jersey Road Woollahra
Sydney 2025
Ph: +61 02 9327 2292
Email: modelsearch@chicmanagement.com.au
Web: chicmanagement.com.au

Priscilla's Model Management
Country: Australia
1/25 Challis Ave Potts Point
Sydney 2011
Ph: 61 2 9332 2422
Web: priscillas.com.au

Country: Australia
Level 2, 4-14 Foster Street Surrey Hills, NSW
Sydney 2010
Ph: +61 02 8217 0111
Email: joseph@chadwickmodels.com
Web: chadwickmodels.com

EMG Models
Country: Australia
19A Boundary Street Level 5
Suite 508, Rushbutters Bay
Sydney 2011
Ph: +612 8302 2900
Email: info@emgmodels.com
Web: emgmodels.com

Sao Paulo

Ford Models Brasil
Country: Brazil
Rua Fidencio Ramos 195-Terreo
Sao Paulo 04551-010
Ph: +55 11 3049 8833
Web: fordmodels.com.br

Kee Mod
Country: Brazil
Avenida 9 de Julho 5328 – Jardim Paulista
Sao Paulo 01434-000
Ph: + 55 11 3051 5191

TEN Model Management
Country: Brazil
Rua Iguatemi, 448 -1' Andar Itaim Bibi
Sao Paulo 01451-010
Ph: +55 11 3702 1313
Email: ten@tenmodelmgt.com.br
Web: tenmodelmgt.com.br

Way Model Management
Country: Brazil
Av. Reboucas, 3642 Jd Paulistano
Sao Paulo 05402-600
Ph: +55 11 2827 5500
Email: waymodel@waymodel.com.br
Web: waymodel.com.br

ELO Management
Country: Brazil
Rua Groenlandia, 508 - Jardim Paulista
Sao Paulo 01434-000
Ph: 11 5083-7738
Email: contato@elomanagement.com
Web: elomanagement.com

Joy Model Management
Country: Brazil Rua Suzano, 88
Sao Paulo 01435-030
Ph: +55 11 2592-8747
Web: joymodelmanagement.com

Mega Model Brasil
Country: Brazil
Av. Tajurás #9 - Cidade Jardim
Sao Paulo
Ph: +55 11 3818 4800
Email: renato.guedes@megamodelbrasil.com.br
Web: megamodelbrasil.com.br

Copenhagen

1st Option Model Management
Country: Denmark Gothersgade 3 1st floor
Copenhagen 1123
Ph: +45 70 26 26 44
Email: info@1stoption.dk
Web: 1stoption.dk

2PM Model Management
Country: Denmark
Vaernedamsvej 16
Copenhagen, V 1619
Ph: +45 3376 6262
Web: 2pm.dk

Elite Copenhagen
Country: Denmark
Bredgade 23b 4th Floor
Copenhagen 1260
Ph: +45 33 15 1414
Web: elitemodelmanagement.dk

Scoop Models
Country Denmark
Laederstraede 9
Copenhagen, K 1201
Phone: +45 33 14 10 13
Email: info@scoopmodels.com
Web: scoopmodels.com

Unique Denmark
Country: Denmark
Snaregade 12 2nd Floor
Copenhagen K, 1205
Ph: +45 33 12 00 55
Email: scout@unique.dk
Web: unique.dk

Shanghai

Esee Model Management
Country: China
5/F, Building 1 No. 751
South Huangpi Road
Shanghai 200020
Ph: +8621 5301 0642
Web: eseemodel.com

Huayi Brothers Fashion Group
Country: China
9A, Lane 294 Xinhua Rd 200051
Shanghai 200051
Ph: +86 21 60899761
Email: info.fashion@huayimedia.com
Web: huayibrothersfashion.com

Milan

2Morrow Model
Country: Italy
Via Enrico Tazzoli, 11
Milan 20154
Ph: +39 0245498660
Email: agency@2morrowmodel.com
Web: 2morrowmodel.com

D'Management Group
Country: Italy
13 via Forcella
Milan 20144
Ph: +39 02 8942 1377
Email: info@dmanagementgroup.com
Web: dmanagementgroup.com

Elite Milan
Country: Italy
Via Tortona 35
Milan 20144
Ph: +39 02 46 75 21
Email: elitemilano@elitemodel.it
Web: elitemodel.it

IMG Milano
Country: Italy
C.SO Di Porta Romana 20
Milan 20122
Ph: +39 02 3657 6550
Web: imgmodels.com

Fashion Model
Via Guglielmo Silva, 40
Milan 20149
Italy
Ph: +39 02 48 08 61
Email: info@fashionmodel.it
Web: fashionmodel.it

MP Management
Country: Italy
Via Lombardini 10
Milan 20143
Ph: +39 02 49 68 84 00
Web: mpmanagement.com

Next Milan
Country: Italy
Via Pontaccio 10
Milan 20121
Ph: +39 02 303 5021
Web: nextmodels.com

Why Not Model Management
Country: Italy
Via Zenale 9
Milan 20123
Ph: +39 02 48 53 31
Email: whynot@whynotmodels.com
Web: whynotmodels.com

Women Milan
Country: Italy
Via Savona 58
Milan 20143
Ph: +39 0 2477 195 57
Web: womenmanagement.com

Cape Town

Boss Models
Country: South Africa
164 Bree Street
Cape Town 8001
Ph: 21 27 424 0224
Email: capetown@bossmodel.co.za
Web: bossmodels.co.za

Ice Model Management
Country: South Africa
160 Sir Lowry Road, Woodstock H102
The Hills, Buchanan Square
Cape Town 7925
Ph: +27 0 21 423 2244
Email: ice@icemodels.co.za
Web: icemodels.co.za